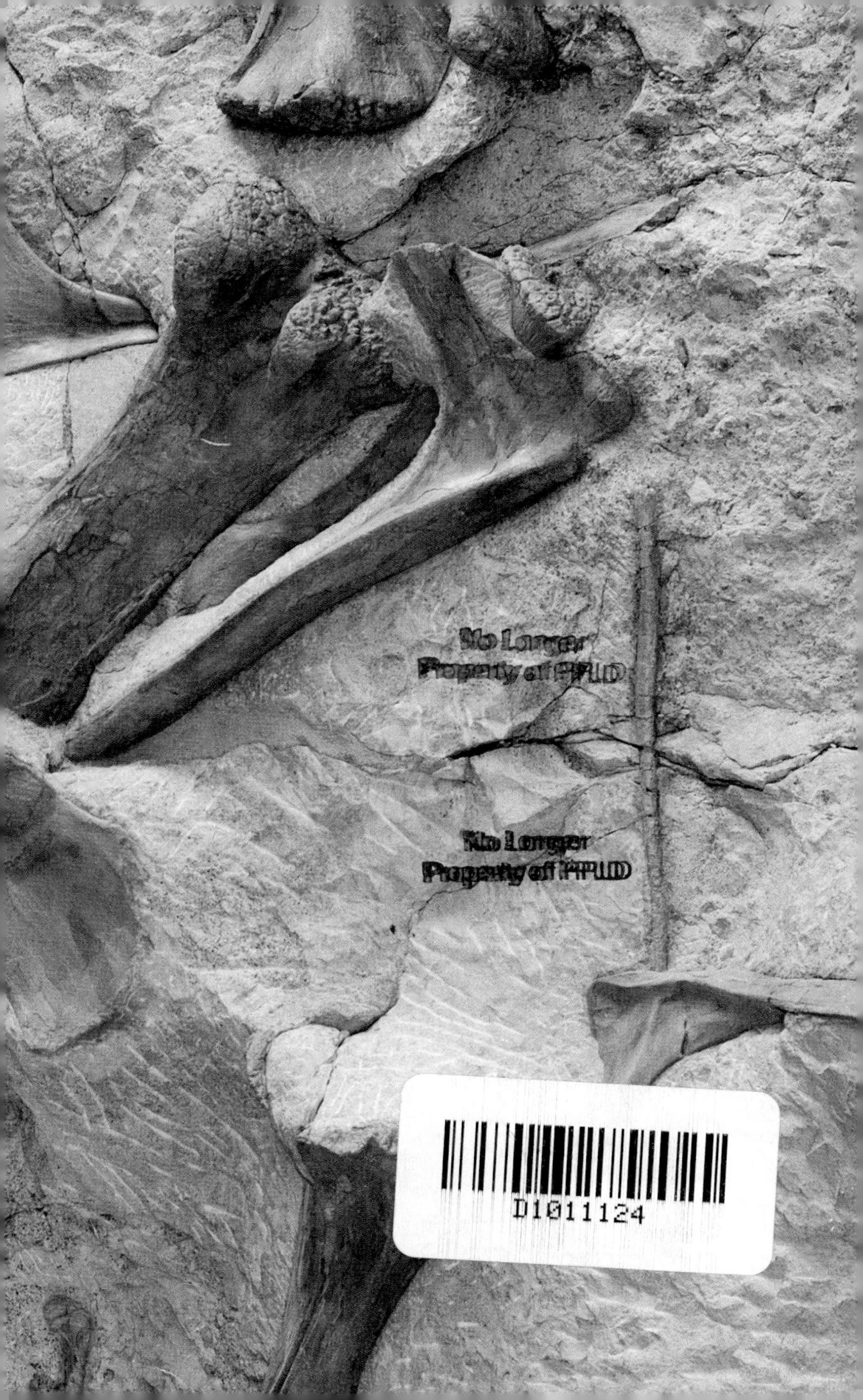

No Longer
Property of PPLD

Mysteries of the Fossil Dig

Mysteries

of the

Fossil
Dig

How Paleontologists Learn About Dinosaurs

By Pamela Rushby

NATIONAL GEOGRAPHIC

WASHINGTON D.C.

One of the world's largest nonprofit scientific and educational organizations, the National Geographic Society was founded in 1888 "for the increase and diffusion of geographic knowledge." Fulfilling this mission, the Society educates and inspires millions every day through its magazines, books, television programs, videos, maps and atlases, research grants, the National Geographic Bee, teacher workshops, and innovative classroom materials. The Society is supported through membership dues, charitable gifts, and income from the sale of its educational products. This support is vital to National Geographic's mission to increase global understanding and promote conservation of our planet through exploration, research, and education.

For more information, please call
1-800-NGS-LINE (647-5463) or write to the following address:
National Geographic Society
1145 17th Street N.W.
Washington, D.C. 20036-4688
U.S.A.

For information about special discounts for bulk purchases, please contact
National Geographic Books Special Sales at ngspecsales@ngs.org

Visit the Society's Web site: www.nationalgeographic.com

Copyright © 2006 National Geographic Society

Text revised from *Dinosaur Detectives* in the National Geographic Windows on Literacy program from National Geographic School Publishing, © 2004 National Geographic Society

All rights reserved. Reproduction of the whole or any part of the contents without written permission from the publisher is prohibited.

Published by National Geographic Society. Washington, D.C. 20036

Design by Project Design Company

Printed in the United States

Library of Congress Cataloging-in-Publication Data

Rushby, Pamela.
  Mysteries of the fossil dig : how paleontologists learn about dinosaurs / by Pamela Rushby.
    p. cm.
  Includes index.
  ISBN-13: 978-0-7922-5953-4 (library binding)
  ISBN-10: 0-7922-5953-X (library binding)
  1. Paleontology--Methodology. I. Title.
  QE721.R87 2006
  567.9--dc22

2006016330

Photo Credits
Front Cover: © Louie Psihoyos/ Corbis; Spine: © Louie Psihoyos/ Corbis; Endpaper: © Dick Durrance II/ National Geographic Image Collection; 2-3: © Louie Psihoyos/ Corbis; 6: © Jim Zuckerman/ Corbis; 7: © Peter Larson/ Black Hill Institute of Geological Research; 8: © Louie Psihoyos/ Corbis; 11: © O. Louis Mazzatenta/ National Geographic Image Collection; 12, 13: © Louie Psihoyos/ Corbis; 14: © Philippe Plailly/ Science Photo Library; 16-17: © Richard T. Nowitz/ Corbis18: © Jonathan Blair/ Corbis; 19: © The Natural History Museum; 20-21: © The Field Museum; 21 (top): © National Geographic Society; 22: © The Natural History Museum; 23: © Michael S. Yamashita/ Corbis; 24-25: © Larry Shaffer/ Black Hill Institute of Geological Research; 26-27: © New Moon/Panoramic Images/ National Geographic Image Collection; 27 (bottom): © The Natural History Museum; 28: © John Cancalosi/ Still Pictures; 30 (left): © Raymond Gehman/ National Geographic Image Collection; 30-31: © Kevin Schafer/ Still Pictures; 32: Getty Images; 34: Matthew Groves/ The Field Museum; 35: © DK Images; Illustrations by Luke Jurevicius.

Contents

A recreation of *Tyrannosaurus rex* shows what this dinosaur looked like when it was alive.

An Amazing Discovery

Sue Hendrickson was hiking in South Dakota one summer morning in 1990. As Sue walked along the base of a cliff, she noticed strange markings on the rock face. When she took a closer look, Sue saw that the markings

Sue Hendrickson found fossils in South Dakota.

looked a lot like rib bones, only much bigger!

Sue knew a lot about dinosaur bones. She thought these bones might belong to a *Tyrannosaurus rex*, a huge meat-eating dinosaur. She called in the professionals. She called in the dinosaur detectives.

This huge *Brachiosaurus* skeleton stands in a museum in Germany.

Chapter 1

All About Dinosaurs

Dinosaurs lived on Earth millions of years ago. They lived in a time called the Mesozoic era. If you look at the chart on the next page, you will see that the Mesozoic era lasted for 183 million years. Dinosaurs died out long before the first humans appeared on Earth.

If no one has ever seen a dinosaur, how do we know what they looked like? How do we know how big they were or what they ate? We have learned about dinosaurs and the world they lived in from the work of scientists called paleontologists.

Paleontologists study plants and animals that lived millions of years ago. They do this by examining fossils, or the hardened remains of plants and animals that lived long ago. Fossils contain clues to the past. Paleontologists try to decipher these clues and make sense of the past. These scientists are dinosaur detectives.

History of Earth

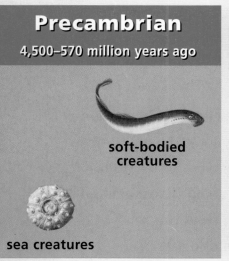

Precambrian
4,500–570 million years ago

soft-bodied
creatures

sea creatures

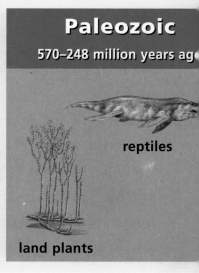

Paleozoic
570–248 million years ago

reptiles

land plants

This 120-million-year-old fossil shows that dragonflies lived during the Mesozoic era.

Mesozoic

248–65 million years ago

dinosaurs

flowering plants

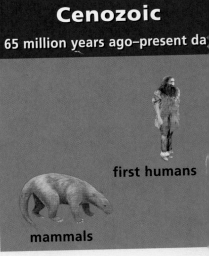

Cenozoic

65 million years ago–present da

first humans

mammals

Fossil Finds

Dinosaur bones have been found all over the world. However, bones are not the only dinosaur fossils. Footprints, eggs, and even dinosaur droppings have been discovered, too. More fossils are found each year.

Not all fossils are bones. These fossils are dinosaur eggs.

Most dinosaur remains have been found in remote places, far from towns. Often they have been found by accident. Someone just happened to notice something unusual in the ground. Finding a dinosaur bone is like uncovering the first clue to a mystery.

This re-creation shows what a baby dinosaur might have looked like inside its egg.

Looking for Clues

When dinosaur bones are discovered, paleontologists are called in to excavate, or dig up, the bones. Digging up dinosaur bones is dirty, time-consuming work. The bones are not always found lying neatly together on top of the ground. The bones can be spread over a wide area. Most bones are embedded, or stuck, in hard rock with only a small amount of the bone showing. The paleontologists need to figure out how to dig them safely out of the rock.

A paleontologist uses his tools to uncover a dinosaur bone that is embedded in rock.

In the Field

The paleontologists mark off the discovery area, or site, working in small sections at a time. They place pegs in the ground, marking the location of bones that have already been found. Then the whole site is divided into squares with string, making a grid.

The paleontologists use the grid to make a map. Everything they find will be recorded on the map. This information will help the paleontologists when they try to figure out how to put the dinosaur's bones together.

Paleontologists set up a string grid to help them map the location of the bones.

The paleontologists start digging in the squares that seem likely to contain bones. They use picks and shovels to move soil out of the way. Then they use brushes to carefully remove dirt from around the bones they find.

It takes a team of skilled paloentolgists to unearth a dinosaur skelton.

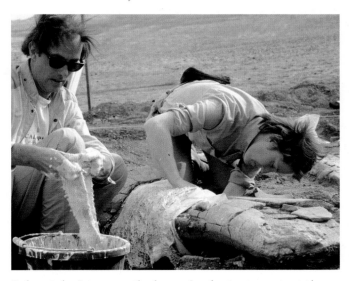
Paleontologists wrap the bones in plaster to protect them when they are being moved to the museum.

Many dinosaur bones are fragile. They break easily when you lift them out of the ground. To avoid breaking the bones, paleontologists dig around them. Then they wrap the bones and the surrounding rock with cloth soaked in wet plaster. When the plaster hardens, it forms a cast. The plaster cast protects the bones as they are taken out of the ground. The bones are then sent to a museum where they will be studied further.

In the Museum

When the bones reach the museum, they are removed from the plaster and cleaned. If a bone is still embedded in rock, it can be removed in different ways. Sometimes a weak acid is used to dissolve the rock.

Pieces of rock are carefully removed from the teeth of a *Tyrannosaurus rex.*

Most of the time, however, a special drill or dentist tools are used to chip away the rock. The paleontologists are careful not to damage the bones in any way. It can take years to remove all the rock from a dinosaur skeleton.

By looking at these bones, scientists know that this dinosaur was a *Tyrannosaurus rex*.

Chapter 3

Detectives at Work

Once the bones have been cleaned, the dinosaur detectives can start making sense of the clues. The size of a hipbone, for example, can tell a paleontologist how big a dinosaur was. The bone can also help the scientists figure out how much a dinosaur weighed.

Fossil teeth and claws provide clues to what a dinosaur ate. When paleontologists find dinosaur bones

This sharp claw belonged to a meat-eating dinosaur called an *Allosaurus.*

with sharp claws, they know they have found a meat-eating dinosaur. The dinosaur would have used the sharp claws to catch its prey. Plant-eating dinosaurs did not have a need for sharp claws.

Making sense of the clues is much harder when a new species, or type, of dinosaur is discovered. Paleontologists compare the recently discovered bones to other fossils that they know more about. They look to see how the bones from the newly discovered species are similar to other dinosaurs.

A metal frame supports this model of a *Tyrannosaurus rex.*

Paleontologists then try to figure out how the bones fit together to make a skeleton. Often, pieces of the skeleton are missing. The dinosaur detectives need to guess what the missing bones might look like.

When you see a dinosaur skeleton in a museum, you are not usually seeing real bones. The fossils are far too fragile and rare to go on display. Museum workers make exact copies of the real bones. Then they attach the copies to a supporting metal frame.

A skeleton can show the shape of a dinosaur, but it doesn't show what the whole dinosaur looked like. To find that out, the dinosaur detectives need to look for more clues.

Marks on the bones can show how the muscles were attached. When paleontologists know how the bones and muscles worked together, they can get a much better idea of what a dinosaur looked like. However, the color of its skin remains a mystery. No one really knows what colors dinosaurs were.

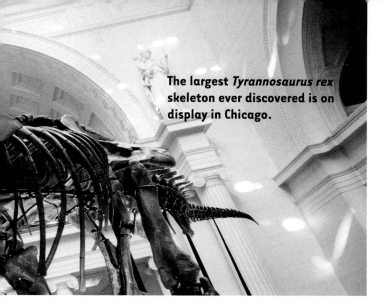

The largest *Tyrannosaurus rex* skeleton ever discovered is on display in Chicago.

These re-creations show what paleontologist think various dinosaur species looked like.

Chapter 4

Detecting the Past

Paleontologists can also use fossils to learn about the world the dinosaurs lived in. Leaf fossils, for example, show what kind of plants grew when the dinosaurs were alive. Bones from other animals provide clues, too. They show what other kinds of animals were alive during that time.

The position of a dinosaur's bones when they are discovered can provide clues, too. If the bones are scattered over a wide area, for example, it's a clue that the dinosaur may

Plant fossils show what plants grew when the dinosaurs lived.

Ferns grew during
dinosaur times.

have died in the water. This clue helps
paleontologists know that an area that is now
desert may have once been covered by water.

Paleontologists use many different tools to
help them create a picture of a world very,

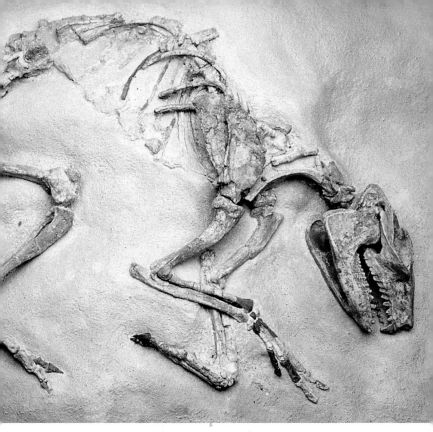

This skeleton was found in one piece of rock.

very far in the past. But the most important tools that paleontologists use are their minds. They use their intelligence and imagination to make sense of fossil clues and unlock secrets of the past.

Paleontologists spend many hours trying to imagine how dinosaur bones fit together.

Solving the Mystery

When the dinosaur detectives arrived in South Dakota, they excavated the bones that Sue Hendrickson found. Then they took the bones to a museum to be studied. The bones belonged to the largest *Tyrannosaurus rex* that had ever been found. Paleontologists nicknamed the dinosaur after the woman who found it. They called the dinosaur "Sue."

Paleontologists agreed that dinosaur Sue would have been terrifying when it was alive. Sue was 41 feet long and more than 13 feet tall. The scariest thing about the dinosaur may have been its huge skull. It measured

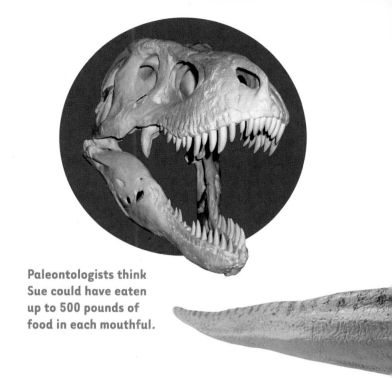

Paleontologists think Sue could have eaten up to 500 pounds of food in each mouthful.

more than five feet long and had 58 very large teeth.

Paleontologists were able to determine that Sue died over 65 million years ago. They think the dinosaur died of old age. But there are still many things about Sue that paleontologists don't know. For example, they don't know if Sue was male or female. They don't know the color of its skin.

The work of the dinosaur detectives isn't finished yet. There are still many dinosaur fossils out there waiting to be discovered. Many mysteries about life long ago still need to be solved.

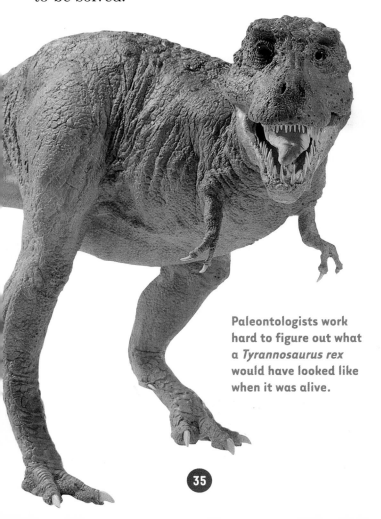

Paleontologists work hard to figure out what a *Tyrannosaurus rex* would have looked like when it was alive.

How to Write an A+ Report

1. Choose a topic.
- Find something that interests you.
- Make sure it is not too big or too small.

2. Find sources.
- Ask your librarian for help.
- Use many different sources: books, magazine articles, and websites.

3. Gather information.
- Take notes. Write down the big ideas and interesting details.
- Use your own words.

4. Organize information.
- Sort your notes into groups that make sense.

- Make an outline. Put your groups of notes in the order you want to write your report.

5. Write your report.

- Write an introduction that tells what the report is about.

- Use your outline and notes as you write to make sure you say everything you want to say in the order you want to say it.

- Write an ending that tells about your report.

- Write a title.

6. Revise and edit your report.

- Read your report to make sure it makes sense.

- Read it again to check spelling, punctuation, and grammar.

7. Hand in your report!

Glossary

embedded	surrounded by or stuck in
excavate	to dig out of the ground
fossil	the hardened remains of a living thing that died millions of years ago
fragile	easily broken
Mesozoic era	a time between 248 million years ago and 65 million years ago
paleontologist	a scientist who studies plant and animal fossils to learn more about the past
prey	an animal hunted by another animal for food
skeleton	the framework of bones in the body of an animal or a person
site	the place where something is found
species	a group of living things that are the same in many ways
Tyrannosaurus rex	a large, meat-eating dinosaur that walked on two legs

Further Reading

• Books •

Barrett, Paul. *National Geographic Dinosaurs.* Washington, DC: National Geographic Society, 2001. Ages 9-12, 192 pages.

Bausum, Ann. *Dragon Bones and Dinosaur Eggs: A Photobiography of Explorer Roy Chapman Andrews.* Washington, DC: National Geographic Society, 2000. Ages 9-12, 64 pages.

Parsons, Jane, ed. *Dinosaur Encyclopedia.* New York, NY: DK Publishing, 2001. Ages 9-12, 376 pages.

Sloan, Christopher. *Feathered Dinosaurs.* Washington, DC: National Geographic Society, 2000. Ages 9-12, 64 pages.

Sloan, Christopher. *SuperCroc and the Origin of Crocodiles.* Washington, DC: National Geographic Society, 2002. Ages 9-12, 64 pages.

• Websites •

National Geographic Society
http://www.nationalgeographic.com/dinorama/

Zoom Dinosaurs
http://www.enchantedlearning.com/subjects/dinosaurs/

San Diego Natural History Museum
http://www.sdnhm.org/kids/dinosaur/index.html

US Geological Survey
pubs.usgs.gov/gip/dinosaurs/

University of California Museum of Paleontology
www.ucmp.berkeley.edu/diapsids/dinosaur.html

Dinosaur Sue:
The Field Museum
http://www.fieldmuseum.org/sue/index.html/

Index